Now You Know
Christmas

Now You Know Christmas

DOUG LENNOX

THE DUNDURN GROUP
TORONTO

Editor: Barry Jowett
Copy editor: Jennifer Gallant
Design: Alison Carr
Printer: Webcom

Library and Archives Canada
Cataloguing in Publication

Lennox, Doug
    Now you know Christmas / Doug Lennox.

ISBN 978-1-55002-745-7

1. Christmas--Miscellanea. I. Title.

GT4985.L45 2007   394.2663
C2007-903567-1

      1   2   3   4   5
     11   10   09   08   07

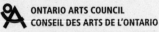

Conseil des Arts **Canada Council**
du Canada **for the Arts**

ONTARIO ARTS COUNCIL
CONSEIL DES ARTS DE L'ONTARIO
an Ontario government agency | un organisme du gouvernement de l'Ontario

Canada

We acknowledge the support of The Canada Council for the Arts and the Ontario Arts Council for our publishing program. We also acknowledge the financial support of the Government of Canada through the Book Publishing Industry Development Program and The Association for the Export of Canadian Books, and the Government of Ontario through the Ontario Book Publishers Tax Credit program, and the Ontario Media Development Corporation.

Care has been taken to trace the ownership of copyright material used in this book. The author and the publisher welcome any information enabling them to rectify any references or credits in subsequent editions.

J. Kirk Howard, President

Printed and bound in Canada.
Printed on recycled paper.

www.dundurn.com

Dundurn Press
3 Church Street, Suite 500
Toronto, Ontario, Canada
M5E 1M2

Gazelle Book Services Ltd
White Cross Mills
High Town, Lancaster,
England, LA1 4XS

Dundurn Press
2250 Military Road
Tonawanda, NY, U.S.A.
14150

Now You Know Christmas

Contents

Preface

Some Christmas books are fireside books. They're written so that grownups can sit in their living rooms with their families, reading tales of holiday merriment beside a fireplace (often artificial nowadays).

This is not one of those books. While the hope is that you will enjoy *Now You Know Christmas* tremendously, and that it will add a little something to your holiday, it was not written to be a "Christmas classic."

This book is for those who celebrate Christmas each year, and who every once in a while stop to wonder why we do some of the things we do and why we believe some of the things we believe. It is for people who wonder what lies beneath the most popular and celebrated holiday in the world.

Why, for example, do we kiss under the mistletoe? It seems like a completely illogical tradition. Why do we say "Merry Christmas" instead of "Happy Christmas"? Why does an obese man come down our chimneys and stuff candies and toys in a sock? (Or for that matter, why would we eat candies we found in a sock?) And why would three supposedly wise men give a baby gold, frankincense, and myrrh — gifts that a baby couldn't possibly have any use for?

It's a book for the curious. It's a book for people like me. You can certainly sit in front of a fireplace — real or simulated — and read aloud directly from this book. But I have a hunch you'd much rather fill your head with some of these answers, hide the book underneath your mattress, and then entertain your friends and family at Christmas dinner with your astonishing knowledge of all things Christmas. Perhaps you can start by telling them how long you'll be able to store that fruitcake Aunt Edna gave you as a gift.

Doug Lennox, 2007

Santa Claus, St. Nicholas & Other Gift-Bringers

Who invented Santa Claus?

"Santa Claus" is a figure who developed over the years, originally taking the form of St. Nicholas. But the Santa we know today largely developed under the guidance of a group of New York writers and historians known as "the Knickerbockers." The group included Washington Irving, Clement C. Moore, and James Fennimore Cooper.

The Knickerbockers played a major role in shaping the way Americans celebrated Christmas, and in the early 1800s, they went to work telling stories of a great gift-bringer who was considerably different from the St. Nicholas people had known. They drew on the Dutch tradition of Sinterklaas, and slowly evolved that name into "Santa Claus." They also gave Santa many of the attributes we know today: the jolly demeanour, the plump belly, the fur suit. They also told us that Santa came down our chimneys and rode in a sleigh pulled by reindeer.

Some have cynically suggested that the Knickerbockers and other social elites created Santa Claus so that poor people would stop knocking on their doors looking for handouts at Christmas, and would instead stay in their own homes staring at their fireplaces in greedy anticipation. But in reality, the group was eager to change Christmas from a time of drinking and carousing into a more family-centred holiday. They also wanted to create a distinctly American — or, more accurately, non-British — holiday.

Is it true that a soft drink company created the modern image of Santa Claus?

Many have credited the Coca-Cola Company with creating the modern image of Santa Claus in his red suit with white trim and black boots. Even Coca-Cola itself celebrated the seventy-fifth anniversary of its creation of the image in 2006. It all stems from a series of ads featuring illustrations by Haddon Sundblom used by the company between 1931 and 1964.

In reality, the modern image of Santa Claus had been around for decades before Sundblom's illustrations saw the light of day. Thomas Nast began illustrating Santa in the 1860s and depicted him as a jolly, rotund character in a red suit with white trim, with a big white beard. While the early Nast illustrations showed us an elf-like Santa, the figure later grew to adult size. By the early 1900s, early filmmakers were presenting a Santa looking very much like our modern Santa in both costume and stature. And more than a decade before the Coca-Cola ads, Norman Rockwell's *Saturday Evening Post* illustrations were showing us that the image of Santa we know today was already well on its way to being the standard.

What Coca-Cola does deserve credit for is turning Santa into one of the greatest pitchmen in the history of advertising. While Santa had been used only sporadically in advertising until that point, Coca-Cola showed the world that the beloved figure could become a shameless huckster.

In what country is the North Pole located?

The true North Pole — the one at the top of the world — is located in international waters. Russia attempted to lay claim to the North Pole in 2001, but that claim was contested by several nations, and to date, no one has planted their flag on Santa's front lawn.

The magnetic North Pole — which is constantly moving — is currently located to the west of Canada's Ellesmere Island. While few people outside Canada believe that this is Santa's home, Canada Post accepts mail addressed to Santa care of "North Pole, Canada."

Two American towns have tried to attract the attention of Santa-seekers by adopting the name "North Pole." North Pole, New York, did so hoping to entice tourists — and they've been successful thanks to the theme park "Santa's Workshop." And North Pole, Alaska, adopted its name in 1953 in the hopes that it would help attract a toymaker to set up shop in the community. To date, no toy company has grabbed that brass ring.

Do all Christmas celebrants believe Santa lives at the North Pole?

The notion that Santa Claus lives at the North Pole was popularized in the nineteenth century by writers such as Washington Irving and Horatio Algiers, as well as by artist Thomas Nast. But while most who have adopted Santa as their Christmas gift-giver believe his home is in the North Pole, the Finns would beg to differ.

In the 1920s, Finnish radio star "Uncle Markus" Rautio declared that Santa lives on Finland's Korvatunturi ("Mount Ear" or "Ear Fell"). This mountain is shaped like an ear and is said to be Santa's ear, through which he listens to hear whether children are being naughty or nice.

Finnish children immediately latched onto the proclamation, and soon other countries began accepting Santa's Finnish citizenship.

Who holds St. Nicholas as their patron saint?

While best known as the patron saint of children — hence his association with Christmas gift-giving — Nicholas is also the patron saint of sailors, students, vagabonds, and pawnbrokers.

The latter association ultimately led to the universal symbol of pawnbrokers: three gold balls hanging above a pawnshop's door. The symbol represents three bags of gold, stemming from the legend in which Nicholas saved three young women from a life of prostitution by throwing bags of gold into their home.

Did St. Nicholas ever celebrate Christmas?

While legends of Nicholas's generosity have been tied to Christmas and have been the basis for some of our holiday traditions, there is no evidence that Nicholas himself ever took part in Christmas celebrations. In fact, for most of his life, Christmas wasn't even officially celebrated by the Church itself. The first recorded celebration by Rome was in A.D. 336, a mere seven years before Nicholas passed away.

Even in death, Nicholas was not tied to Christmas until the eleventh or twelfth century.

Is Nicholas still a saint?

In 1968, the Roman Catholic Church removed forty saints from its roster. Nicholas was not among these decanonized saints. However, the Church did remove his feast from the universal liturgical calendar, meaning that celebrating Nicholas's feast day was no longer required by Roman Catholic law.

The Church took pains to emphasize that Nicholas and others who suffered a similar fate had not been demoted, saying "Saints who lost their places or whose feast days were demoted from universal to optional in the new edition of the liturgical calendar are still to be venerated as they were before the calendar's updating."

Does Mrs. Claus have a first name?

Yes. In fact, she seems to go by different names depending on where you live. In Switzerland, she is known as "Lucy." In Austria, "Nikolofrau." And in the Netherlands, "Molly Grietja."

Movies and stories have often given her a name. Angela Lansbury played her as "Anna" in the 1996 TV movie *Mrs. Santa Claus*, while Katherine Lee Bates (better known as the lyricist responsible for "America the Beautiful") named her "Goody" in the story "Goody Santa Claus on a Sleigh Ride." In the Rankin and Bass TV special *Santa Claus is Comin' to Town*, Mrs. Claus answers to the name "Jessica."

Despite the many names she goes by, there appears to be only one Mrs. Claus, so there's no need to worry about any indiscretions on the part of Santa.

When did Santa first appear in department stores?

J.W. Parkinson's department store in Philadelphia was the first to invite Santa to make a personal appearance in 1841. It seems to have been an exclusive arrangement, because Santa didn't appear at any other stores until 1890, when he graced the Boston Store in Brockton, Massachusetts. Since then, Santa has become a fixture at malls everywhere during the holiday season, taking gift orders from children and posing for pictures.

How many letters to Santa does the post office process each year?

Canada Post, claiming that Santa Claus lives near the magnetic North Pole, which lies within Canadian territory, has a special postal code for Santa's home: H0H 0H0. Approximately 1 million letters come to this postal code each year from Canada and around the world, and Canada Post claims that they answer each letter in the language in which it was written.

Meanwhile, the post office in North Pole, Alaska, processes roughly 120,000 letters to Santa each year. U.S. numbers are more difficult to track, since post offices in different communities have their own letters-to-Santa programs.

Gift-Bringers Not Named "Santa"

While Santa Claus gets the most press in many countries around the globe, he doesn't have a monopoly on gift-giving. The following are the gift-bringers in various countries:

Brazil	Papai Noel
Denmark	Julemand
England	Father Christmas
Finland	Joulupukki
France	Pere Noel
Germany	Christkindl
Netherlands	Sinterklaas
Italy	Old Befana
Phillipines	The Three Kings
Russia	Baboushka
Spain	The Three Kings
Sweden	Jultomten

But Santa isn't the only gift-bringer with a lot of reading to do in December. In the United Kingdom, the Royal Mail receives 750,000 letters to Father Christmas.

When did NORAD begin tracking Santa's Christmas Eve journey?

In 1955, NORAD began tracking Santa Claus as the result of an error in a newspaper ad. A Sears store in Colorado had printed an ad telling children that they could call their Santa Hotline in order to get an update on Santa's progress in his journey around the world. Unfortunately, the phone number in the ad was wrong, and turned out to be the phone number for NORAD. Rather than rain on the kiddies' Christmas parade, NORAD operators honed in on the big guy so that they could advise callers of Santa's location.

This began a Santa-tracking tradition, and extended beyond the telephone to include updates provided for television and radio stations.

In recent years, NORAD has brought Santa into the Internet age with a website devoted to following his journey. Web-surfers visiting www.noradsanta.org receive frequent updates that include visuals of Santa as he visits countries around the world.

How fast would Santa Claus need to travel in order to visit all the children in the world on Christmas Eve?

If we assume Santa delivers presents at night — between 8 p.m. when kids go to bed and 6 a.m. when they're banging on their parents' doors begging to open presents — Santa has a ten-hour period in which to deliver the goods. However, if he plays his cards right and starts at the International Date Line and heads from east to west, he gains an extra twenty-four hours, for a grand total of thirty-four hours of delivery time.

We'll assume that there are 800 million homes to visit (2 billion children, with 2.5 children per household). He has 160 million miles to cover. We're told that it's impossible to travel at the speed of light, but it *is* theoretically possible to travel at just under the speed of light. If Santa travels at 99.99999999 percent of the speed of light, he can make it to every child's home in around eight minutes and twenty seconds. That leaves him with thirty-three hours, fifty-one minutes, and forty seconds to put presents under trees, fill stockings, and consume his complimentary milk and cookies. He'll have to work quickly, though, because that only leaves him with 0.0000000423 seconds at each house.

Now, at near-lightspeed, the reindeer would likely burst into flames, but presumably Santa has come up with some special protection to avoid this catastrophe.

20

Where did the name "Kris Kringle" come from?

Although "Kris Kringle" is a name now synonymous with "Santa Claus," Kris Kringle's origins predate the Santa tradition.

"Christkindl" was an early gift-bringer who supplanted St. Nicholas in Germany, Switzerland, and Austria. But Christkindl differed from other gift-bringers in that he was the Christ Child himself.

The name made it way across the Atlantic and morphed into "Kris Kringle." As the various gift-bringers stepped aside in the face of the growing popularity of Santa Claus in the 1800s, "Kris Kringle" began to be another name for Santa.

Which gift-bringer came first: Father Christmas or Santa Claus?

The name "Father Christmas" predates "Santa Claus" by a fair margin. The earliest references to Father Christmas come from the fifteenth century, whereas Santa happened upon the scene in the early nineteenth century. In fact, Father Christmas may have existed long before those earliest records, as it's been said that his origins were pagan.

However, it's worth noting that the Father Christmas we know today changed a great deal because of Santa's influence. Where Father Christmas was once simply a symbol of Christmas merriment, the popularity of Santa Claus as a gift-bringer forced Father Christmas to carry a bag full of toys himself in order to maintain his popularity among British children.

Trees & Other Decorations

When did we start putting fir trees in our living rooms?

The origins of the Christmas tree are murky and have been debated over the years, but we can say with certainty that Germany played a critical role in popularizing the tradition. The German tree seems to have stemmed from a European custom in the Middle Ages. The feast day of Adam and Eve was December 24, and medieval mystery plays marking the occasion featured a paradise tree. The paradise tree soon moved into homes. By 1605, we'd seen the first written description of a fully decorated, indoor Christmas tree in Strasbourg, Germany: "at Christmas they set up fir trees in the parlors and hang upon them roses cut from many-colored paper, apples, wafers, gilt-sugar, sweets, etc."

When were electric lights first sold to adorn Christmas trees?

Biggest and Tallest

- The world's biggest Christmas stocking was made in 2005 by students at the University of Central Arkansas. It measured fifty-three feet long, and the distance from heel to toe was twenty-seven feet.
- Bronner's Christmas Wonderland in Frankenmuth, Michigan, is the world's largest Christmas store, stocking fifty thousand items and featuring a half-mile "Christmas Lane."
- The world's tallest Christmas tree was a eucalyptus tree in Tasmania that was decorated with more than three thousand Christmas lights by environmentalists looking to draw attention to the plight of Tasmania's tall trees. It was eighty metres tall.

As lovely as earlier attempts to light Christmas trees were, candles and oil lamps presented obvious safety concerns. In 1882, three years after Thomas Edison invented the incandescent light bulb, one of his business associates, Edward Johnson, illuminated a tree in his home with eighty small bulbs, and invited the press to witness the historic event. The lights were first mass-produced by General Electric in 1890, and sold for what would have been a hefty sum in those days: twelve dollars a string.

How many trees are cut down each Christmas?

In the United States, anywhere between 30 and 40 million trees are cut down for use as Christmas trees each year. In Europe, the number is between 50 and 60 million. While this apparent carnage has caused some to wonder if the use of real Christmas trees is an environmentally sound practice, the reality is that the overwhelming majority of modern holiday trees come from dedicated Christmas tree farms, and each tree that is harvested for Christmas is replaced by a newly planted tree.

How many Christmas tree fires do firefighters respond to each year?

According to the National Fire Protection Association, there are an average of three hundred Christmas tree fires in the United States annually. Of these, 40 percent are caused by electrical problems, 25 percent by a heat source too close to the tree, and 6 percent by children playing with fire.

Christmas tree fires are particularly dangerous, as a tree can be fully engulfed within a few seconds and can lead to devastating consequences.

Who was the first U.S. president to set up a tree in the White House?

The White House was quick to join the Christmas tree craze when it hit America. Christmas trees had only emerged in the United States in the late 1840s, and by 1856, Franklin Pierce had set up a tree inside the White House.

The tradition of displaying a tree on the White House lawn began many years later under Warren G. Harding in the 1920s.

Not all presidents were so welcoming of the Christmas tree, however. Teddy Roosevelt, a noted conservationist, took a stand against the annual tree massacre by banning Christmas trees at the White House during his presidency.

Why do we hang stockings on Christmas Eve?

The tradition of the stocking stems from a legend associated with St. Nicholas. When Nicholas was Bishop of Myra in the early fourth century, he learned of a nobleman who had fallen on hard times. The man had three daughters, and the young women had no marriage prospects, as their father could offer no dowry. The only option the father could come up with was to sell his daughters into prostitution.

Nicholas came by the family's home one night and threw a bag of gold through a window — enough gold to serve as a dowry for one daughter. The next night, he threw a second bag of gold through the window. But on the third night, the window was closed, so instead Nicholas threw the third daughter's gold down the chimney. According to the legend, the townspeople heard the story and hung stockings by their fireplaces at night in the hopes that they too would catch bags of gold coming down their chimneys.

Where did the Advent calendar originate?

Advent calendars are a relatively new Christmas tradition, originating in the mid-1800s in Germany and Scandinavia. Early Advent calendars were homemade, and featured twenty-four small doors. From December 1 to 24, one door was opened each day to reveal a picture, toy, or candy. The Advent calendar remains to this day in homes around the world, most often taking the form of store-bought cardboard packages with fold-out doors revealing small pieces of chocolate.

Are poinsettias really poisonous?

While poinsettia plants may not make a tasty salad, they are, contrary to a popular belief, not toxic.

The myth of the poison poinsettia seems to stem from the story of a two-year-old child in 1919 who reportedly died shortly after eating parts of a poinsettia plant. However, it was never established that the plant was to blame.

Numerous tests have been done on poinsettia plants over the years, to the point that the American Society of Florists has said that no other consumer plant has ever been tested as much as the poinsettia. But fortunately for your children and your pets — and any drop-by holiday visitors with peculiar eating habits — the poinsettia is virtually harmless.

Why do we hang wreaths?

The Christmas wreath comes from pagan origins in Germany and other parts of Europe, where a wreath of evergreen was used to symbolize eternal life and the coming spring. This was adopted by Christians in the form of the Advent wreath, which differed from the modern Christmas wreath in that it contained candles that would be lit, one by one, as Christmas approached. In the twentieth century, traditional wreaths made from real fir branches or holly were, for the most part, replaced by artificial wreaths.

Why was tinsel once banned in the United States?

Tinsel used to contain lead, and this presented health concerns. So, in the 1960s, it was banned by the United States government. Tinsel makers soon adapted, and removed lead from the decoration. Modern tinsel is made from plastic, which doesn't hang as nicely from tree branches but is a lesser safety concern.

When were Christmas tree ornaments first manufactured and sold?

While it had been customary to decorate Christmas trees for a few centuries, the decorations tended to be hand-made or took the form of candies, cakes, fruits, and flowers. It wasn't until 1880 that the first manufactured Christmas tree ornaments were sold at the Woolworths department store.

Customs & Traditions

Why do we kiss under the mistletoe?

In the Middle Ages, many homes in England displayed a hoop decorated with greenery (including mistletoe) with figures of the Holy Family in the middle. Over the years, the Holy Family disappeared, but the greenery display remained, and this was known as the kissing bough. It was customary to kiss or embrace under the kissing bough. As time went on, the bough got smaller and smaller until a bunch of mistletoe was all that remained.

What is "wassailing"?

Most of us only know the term *wassailing* from the song, "Here We Come a-Wassailing." The tradition of wassailing has vanished over the years, leaving many to wonder what the song is referring to.

The word *wassail* comes from the Anglo-Saxon phrase *waes hael*, meaning "good health" — a phrase offered as a toast when drinking. At Christmastime, wassailers would journey from door to door singing carols in exchange for drinks from a punch bowl. Another tradition had things working the other way around: the wassailers would carry a punch bowl from door to door, offering drinks in exchange for a monetary expression of appreciation. Either way, there was a great deal of drinking to "good health."

Why is the day after Christmas known as "Boxing Day" in many countries?

England, Canada, and other Commonwealth countries celebrate December 26 as a legal holiday known as "Boxing Day." The origins are a bit murky, but most believe that Boxing Day began as a tradition in which apprentices and assistants would, on the day after Christmas, visit their employers' customers seeking monetary gifts as tips for their service throughout the year. They would carry boxes for the collection of these tips.

Another theory has it that Boxing Day began when parish church alms boxes were opened and their contents distributed to poor members of the community.

Whatever the origins, the Boxing Day tradition continues in name only, and has been distanced from its charitable origins. Now,

Quickies
Did you know ...
• that in Poland in the Middle Ages it was believed that a child born on Christmas Day was likely to become a werewolf?
• that Marquette, Michigan, is more likely to experience a white Christmas than Anchorage, Alaska, or Saskatoon, Saskatchewan?
• that it's considered bad luck to throw out the ashes from your yule log on Christmas Day?

Boxing Day has become the beginning of Boxing Week, a time when shoppers can find post-Christmas bargains at stores and malls.

What is the oldest Santa Claus Parade in the world?

In 1905, the world's first Santa Claus Parade was held in Toronto. It was a small affair that year, amounting to a solitary Santa walking from the city's Union Station up Yonge Street to the Eaton's department store. The parade quickly grew and, despite financial difficulties that nearly derailed the event in the 1980s, the Toronto Santa Claus

Parade is still a popular annual tradition that is broadcast around the world.

When was the first Macy's Thanksgiving Day Parade?

The Macy's Thanksgiving Day Parade first made its way through the streets of New York in 1925. Since then, it has become the most famous of all the holiday parades, even figuring prominently in the film *Miracle on 34th Street*. The parade is best known for its giant balloons, many of which take the form of popular cartoon characters.

How did the tradition of the Boar's Head Feast originate?

It is believed that the Boar's Head Feast originated in pagan times when boars would be sacrificed in honour of the Norse fertility god Frey. The tradition was eventually adopted as a Christmas custom in the Middle Ages, though for the most part it died out over time. However, there are still pockets of Christmas celebrants who enjoy a Boar's Head Feast every year.

A less likely story — though infinitely more entertaining — tells us that a student at Queen's College, Oxford, in England founded the feast by accident. During a stroll in Shotover Forest, he was chased by a boar. Having no other means of defence, he shoved his book of Aristotle's writings down the boar's throat. He soon realized that he was going to need his Aristotle back, and so he cut off the poor boar's head and took it back to the college, where he and his fellow students cooked the head and had what was, supposedly, the first ever Boar's Head Feast. While this story is almost certainly more fiction than fact, the feast tradition continues at Queen's College to this day.

Besides a lump of coal, what other consequences might naughty boys and girls face at Christmas?

Kids should count themselves lucky if the punishment for naughty behaviour is a lump of coal at Christmas. In some traditions present and past, corporal punishment has been in vogue.

In most cases, Santa (or another gift-bringer) leaves the dirty work to someone else. In the Netherlands, St. Nicholas is accompanied by Zwarte Piet ("Black Peter"), who brandishes switches and threatens to tie children in a sack and haul them off to Spain. Pére Fouchette in France accompanies Pére Nöel and likewise threatens youngsters with switches. In Austria, Krampus threatens to beat naughty kids with a rod or whip and then stuff them in his basket.

Santa doesn't have a comparable helper in North American tradition, and so in *Children's Friend*, an early book about the jolly man, we're told that Santa leaves a "long, black birchen rod" that parents can use to beat their children. And apparently Santa couldn't rely on parents to do the beatings themselves, for as we see in some of legendary Santa illustrator Thomas Nast's artwork, Santa has been known to carry switches at times.

Who invented the Christmas cracker?

Tom Smith, a London confectioner, invented the Christmas cracker in 1847. The first crackers contained candy and a greeting, and made the familiar cracking noise when pulled open. He soon replaced the candy with toys and other prizes, and his invention quickly caught on. Today, the Christmas cracker is still a tradition in England and Commonwealth countries, and usually contains a toy, a joke, and a tissue-paper hat that revellers are expected to wear for Christmas dinner.

Who began the tradition of the nativity play?

A staple of school and church Christmas pageants today, the nativity scene was first staged in Greccio, Italy, in 1223 by St. Francis of Assissi.

Nativity plays re-enact the birth of Jesus and typically feature the Holy Family, the Wise Men, the shepherds, and one or several angels.

Who invented the pre-Christmas anti-holiday, Festivus?

A 1997 episode of *Seinfeld* introduced the world to the pseudo-holiday of Festivus, and since then, the day has enjoyed a surprising and growing popularity. Celebrated on December 23, Festivus features an aluminum pole (in place of a Christmas tree) and such Festivus dinner activities as "the Airing of Grievances" and "the Feats of Strength." (The latter tradition requires that a celebrant wrestle the head of the household to the floor and pin him or her.)

Although it was *Seinfeld* that first brought Festivus to the masses, the holiday had been an annual tradition of the O'Keefe family for years. *Reader's Digest* columnist Dan O'Keefe created Festivus in 1966. His son, Daniel, would grow up to become a writer on *Seinfeld*, and worked Festivus into a storyline.

What is "Operation Santa Claus"?

Since the 1920s, postal workers in New York City have volunteered to be a part of Operation Santa Claus. Letters written to Santa by American children are read by the workers, who then respond to as many as they can. Each year Operation Santa Claus volunteers respond to roughly two hundred thousand letters.

Season's Greetings! December Holidays

The generic, politically correct phrase "Season's Greetings" has become a common way of including all faiths and traditions in the merriment of December. The following is a list of holidays celebrated in December:

St. Nicholas Day • December 6
Guadalupe Day • December 12
St. Lucia Day • December 13
Hanukkah • An eight-day celebration, the dates of which vary from year to year
Christmas Eve • December 24
Christmas Day • December 25
Boxing Day • December 26
Kwanzaa • December 26 to January 1
New Year's Eve • December 31

How did Vancouver's "Carol Ships" tradition begin?

The Carol Ships have brought the holidays to Vancouver's Coal Harbour since the early 1960s. The tradition began in 1961 with a single ship, the SS *Master*, towing a scow that carried a Christmas tree. Since then, the festivities have expanded to the point where there are now eighty ships, decked out in coloured lights and decorations, carrying forty-five thousand carol singers. The parade of ships takes place each night from

December 1 to 23, and is witnessed by two hundred thousand people annually.

Why do some people celebrate Christmas in December, while others celebrate it in January?

No one can say with certainty what date Jesus was born, and the various churches can't seem to agree. While most of the world celebrates Christmas on December 25, notable exceptions are Armenia and the Ukraine.

The Armenian Church puts greater emphasis on the baptism of Jesus than on his birth, and the date of his baptism is placed on January 6. The Armenian Church in Jerusalem celebrates Christmas thirteen days later, on January 19, because they adhere to the Julian calendar, which is currently thirteen days out of sync with the Gregorian calendar that most of the world follows.

The Ukraine, meanwhile, uses December 25 as the date for Christmas, but because they also remain true to the Julian calendar, their December 25 occurs on our January 7.

What is a "first-footer"?

In many areas of Europe, tradition states that the first person to enter a home on Christmas or at New Year's carries with them great fortune (or lack thereof).

One of the most common English traditions says that the first person to enter a home in the new year should be a dark-haired male. (Although in some places, fair- or red-haired men — or women — are preferable.)

In Greek tradition, the gender or hair colour of the first-footer is irrelevant, but it is felt that the first person to enter a home in the new year brings either good or bad luck. To ensure that it is *good* luck that they bring, the head of the house, upon the first-footer's entrance, will distribute treats to those who are present. After all, if the first-footer's arrival means that everyone gets treats, how can that be anything *but* an indication of good luck?

How many times is Christmas celebrated in Bethlehem each year?

Christmas is celebrated three times a year in Bethlehem. Catholic and Protestant festivities take place on December 24; Orthodox churches celebrate on January 7; and Armenian Christians in Jerusalem observe Christmas on January 19.

When did the Salvation Army begin its kettle campaign?

The sight of Salvation Army officers ringing a bell and standing next to a kettle — awaiting charitable donations — has taken on an iconic status in Christmas tradition. The first Salvation Army kettle was set up in San Francisco in 1891 by Joseph McPhee.

While many Salvation Army officers have abandoned the bell, the kettle remains and continues to help support Christmas charities.

What is Advent?

Advent (which takes its name from the Latin word *adventus*, or "coming") is the period of preparation for the celebration of Christmas. How long Advent lasts depends on who you are. Followers of Eastern churches begin Advent on November 15. Followers of Western churches, meanwhile, begin advent on the Sunday nearest to November 30, which is St. Andrew's Day.

A more secular use of the word defines *Advent* as the period from December 1 to 24 — a period that has been nearly standardized thanks to mass-produced Advent calendars.

Why do we say "Merry Christmas"?

We don't wish each other "Merry New Year," "Merry Birthday," or "Merry Easter," so it strikes some as odd that we call out "Merry Christmas" in December. While the modern definition of the word *merry* suggests joy and celebration, back when the word was first applied to Christmas in the early nineteenth century, it meant "peaceful" or "blessed."

History

Why do we celebrate Christmas on December 25?

There are a number of competing theories as to how Christmas landed on December 25, but the one thing everyone agrees on is that it's highly unlikely that Jesus was actually born on that date.

Most now accept that the choice of December 25 was a response to the popularity of pagan gods who were celebrated on or around the same date. The feast of Sol Invictus, a Roman god, took place on that day, as did the feast of Mithras, an Iranian god whose influence was felt among Roman soldiers. Also, the festival of Saturnalia concluded the day before, on December 24.

Another theory points to a non-pagan reason for the dating of Christmas. It's known that in the early centuries of Christianity, theologians thought there was a good deal of symmetry in the way the world unfolded. It was believed that the world was created on March 25. It was also believed that the Annunciation — the moment when the Virgin Mary learned she was going to give birth to the Son of God — took place on that same date. So, counting nine months from March 25 meant that Jesus was born on December 25.

Why is "Xmas" a short form of "Christmas"?

While many frown upon the use of "Xmas" as an attempt to remove the name "Christ" from the holiday's name, the *X* actually stands for Christ himself. *X* is the Greek letter *chi*, and is the first letter in *Xristos*, the Greek word for "Christ." The Greeks have long used *X* or *chi* as a symbol of Christ.

When was Christmas first celebrated?

Although December 25 was selected by theologians as the date of Christmas early in the second century, there's no evidence that it was actually celebrated until at least the third century.

Early Christians normally didn't bother with celebrating any birthdays, and in the case of Jesus, they would have marked the most important event in his life — his death and subsequent resurrection — but not his birth. (Two of the four Gospels don't even mention Jesus' birth.)

While there is some evidence that Christmas may have been celebrated in the late 200s, the earliest record we have of Christmas being officially celebrated come from Rome in A.D. 336.

How to Make Sure Everyone Forgets Your Birthday...

Famous people who were born on Christmas Day:

1818 • Clara Barton (founder of the American Red Cross)
1899 • Humphrey Bogart (actor)
1907 • Cab Calloway (singer)
1908 • Quentin Crisp (author)
1918 • Anwar Sadat (Egyptian president)
1921 • Steve Allen (comedian)
1924 • Rod Serling (creator and host of *The Twilight Zone*)
1925 • Carlos Castenada (author)
1935 • Richard Penniman, better known as "Little Richard" (singer)
1940 • Phil Spector (music producer)
1946 • Jimmy Buffet (singer-songwriter)
1948 • Barbara Mandrell (singer)
1949 • Sissy Spacek (actress)
1954 • Annie Lennox (singer)
1958 • Rickey Henderson (baseball player)
1960 • Amy Grant (singer)
1965 • Dmitri Mironov (hockey player)

Who was the "Virginia" of "Yes, Virginia, there is a Santa Claus"?

In 1897, Virginia O'Hanlon was an eight-year-old New York schoolgirl. That September, after debating the existence of Santa Claus with her friends, Virginia wrote a letter to the *New York Sun*, asking for a definitive answer on the existence of the jolly man. The *Sun* responded to her letter in the September 21 edition of the paper. Pointing to the goodness and generosity that existed in the world, and to the faith of children like Virginia despite the skepticism surrounding them, the *Sun* argued that yes, there was a Santa Claus.

While the *Sun*'s reply was uncredited at first, the paper later identified Francis Church as the author of the now-legendary editorial.

Did opposing soldiers really stop fighting during the First World War to celebrate Christmas together?

Christmas truces have been common in history, but some of the most dramatic occurred during the first two years of the First World War, when battling armies put aside their differences in honour of the holiday.

The most famous of these incidents took place at Christmas 1914 near Ypres, Belgium. German soldiers began singing Christmas carols in their trenches. Hearing the singing, British troops began singing as well, and soon the two sides left their trenches and met in no man's land — the normally bloody zone between opposing trenches. The foes sang together and exchanged gifts of food and whiskey before returning to their respective positions.

Where does the word *yule* come from?

Scholars disagree over the origins of the word *yule*, but there are two main schools of thought. Many believe that the word derives from the Anglo-Saxon word *Geol*, a pre-Christian feast celebrating the winter solstice.

The other main school of thought points to Scandinavian origins, this time from the word *Juul*, which also was the name for a feast at the winter solstice.

How did the yule log originate?

Those favouring Scandinavian origins for the word *yule* point to the bonfires that took place during the Juul festival. Over time, and the adoption of the tradition as part of the Christian celebration of Christmas, the bonfire shrunk to a single log on the fire.

Is it true that suicide rates climb at Christmas?

The "Christmas blues" are much talked about, and a popular belief is that suicide rates skyrocket during the holiday season. However, that appears to be a myth. A British study in the early 1980s examined a nineteen-year period and found that among men, there was no seasonal variation in the number of suicides, while among women, the suicide rate actually plummeted during December. Meanwhile, multiple American studies in the late 1980s and early 1990s demonstrated that the number of suicides and attempted suicides dips in December. And a 1994 study of suicide rates in Alberta, Canada, over a four-year period found that August was the most likely month for suicide, while December ranked ninth out of twelve months in the number of suicides.

What was the "Bean King"?

In the Middle Ages, it was customary to serve Twelfth Night celebrants cakes, one of which would contain a bean. The lucky person to find a bean in his cake would be named the "Bean King" for the evening.

How did Christmas Island get its name?

The island had appeared on British nautical charts since the early 1600s, but it wasn't until Captain William Mynors of the British East India Company arrived on Christmas Day 1643 that it was finally given a name. Appropriately enough, Mynors's ship was the *Royal Mary*.

The island has been the property of a number of countries since then: Great Britain, Malaya, Japan, and now Australia. Christmas Island boasts 1,600 residents.

When did the first Christmas computer virus attack?

Computer viruses are now commonplace and frequently are tied to significant dates in the calendar year. Christmas is no exception, and there have been a number of

Christmas viruses that have given computer users fits in the Internet age.

Back in 1987, however, computer viruses were virtually unknown to the mass public. But they became a stark reality for users of BITNET, an early communications network, when, at Christmas that year, the "Christmas Tree Virus" — the first ever Christmas-themed virus — infected 350,000 computers. The virus produced a digital Christmas tree and sent it to all of a user's contacts. Infected computers were paralyzed by the attack.

They Said What? Celebrity Quotes about Christmas

"Adults can take a simple holiday for children and screw it up."
— Erma Bombeck

"Is not Christmas the only occasion when one gets drunk *for the sake of the children*?"
— James Cameron

"Christmas in Australia is a gigantic mistake."
— Marcus Clarke

"A Merry Christmas to all my friends except two."
— W.C. Fields

"I stopped believing in Santa Claus when my mother took me to see him in a department store, and he asked me for my autograph."
— Shirley Temple

"The prospect of Christmas appalls me."
— Evelyn Waugh

"Christmas will soon be at our throats."
— P.G. Wodehouse

Christmas in the Bible

What was the Christmas Star?

Trying to find a scientific explanation for the Christmas Star has been an obsession for many over the centuries. Dating Christ's birth is a key to determining what the star was. Using clues from the Bible, the most common opinion seems to be that Jesus was born between 8 and 4 B.C.

Also critical is an understanding that the "three kings" who follow the star in the Christmas story were likely not kings, but rather magi from the East, well-versed in astrology and the significance of the motions of celestial objects.

One theory suggests that the star was a comet, such as the one that was reported in ancient Chinese star maps in

5 B.C. and was, apparently, visible for seventy days. Comets were thought to herald momentous events. Others have speculated that a supernova — an exploding star — attracted the attention of the magi.

Modern scholarship leans towards a conjunction of planets, particularly any conjunction involving the "royal star," Jupiter. The leading candidate seems to be an event in 7 B.C. when Jupiter was eclipsed by the moon in the constellation of Aries — an unusual occurrence that would have had the magi giddy with excitement.

Of course, through all the searching for a scientific explanation, many Christians have held to the belief that the star was a miracle from God, and that searches for a scientific explanation are pointless.

Was Jesus really born in a stable?

The Bible tells us that when Jesus was born, he was laid "in a manger, because there was no room for them in the inn." We've assumed that the manger was in a stable, because that's where mangers are kept.

However, in ancient Israel, mangers were often kept in homes. The homes had two levels — an upper level, where the family dwelled, and a lower level, where animals lived and mangers were kept. The "inn" that had no room may have been the upper dwelling area. The Greek word that is used in the New Testament, *katalyma*, is a general word that can refer to a dwelling area, a guest room, or a lodging. It *could* be translated as "inn," but when the word is used elsewhere in the New Testament, it is clearly referring to a guest room or other such area in a private home — not an inn.

With all this in mind, we can see that it is very possible, if not probable, that what the Bible is telling us is that there was no room in the guest room or dwelling area of the home, and so Mary had to give birth to Jesus and put him in the manger in the area below where the animals were kept.

Does the original manger where Jesus slept still exist?

Most feel that it's unlikely the manger Jesus was laid in after his birth was preserved. However, one church claims that it has the relic. The Church of Santa Maria Maggiore in Rome displays five wooden slats every Christmas Eve. Made from sycamore, these slats, we're told, were the framework for the original manger.

What are swaddling clothes?

The Bible tells us that when he was born, Jesus was wrapped in "swaddling clothes." Swaddling clothes have been used for newborns for millennia — at least as far back as ancient Greece. The swaddling clothes Jesus was wrapped in would have been strips of cloth wrapped tightly around his body. The purpose of swaddling clothes was to immobilize a baby's limbs and promote good posture.

The practice began to be frowned upon in the seventeenth and eighteenth centuries, and today it is uncommon in most of the world to use traditional swaddling clothes.

Who were the Wise Men?

While they came to be known as the "Three Kings" over the centuries, it is most likely that the Wise Men were Persian mystics, possibly originating in Babylon. Such mystics, or magi, would have been likely to find significance in stars, and would have been prime candidates for seeking out a new king of kings if the stars told them that king's birth was coming.

How many Wise Men were there?

We've come to believe that there were three Wise Men, but the Bible never tells us how many Wise Men there were. In fact, early paintings and other images showed as few as two and as many as a dozen Wise Men.

So how did we wind up with three Wise Men as the number of choice? Probably because, somewhere along the line, someone assumed that since there were three gifts — gold, frankincense, and myrrh — there must have been one Wise Man per gift.

Why did the Wise Men bring gold, frankincense, and myrrh as gifts?

At the time of Christ's birth, gold, frankincense, and myrrh were extremely rare and valuable and would have been fitting gifts for any king.

But a story from Marco Polo suggests there may have been greater significance to the gifts. While travelling through Persia, he heard that presenting these three gifts to a newborn would tell you what greatness the child

> ***Quickies***
> **Did you know ...**
> • that, despite what Christmas cards show us, the Bible never says there were animals present at the birth of Christ?
> • that the Wise Men didn't arrive until up to two years after Jesus was born?

possessed. If the child reached for the gold, it indicated that he was an earthly king. If he reached for the frankincense, it suggested he was a god. And if he reached for the myrrh, it suggested he was a mortal man. Reaching for all three demonstrated that the child was a divine king, both god and human.

How did the Wise Men get their traditional names — Melchior, Balthazar, and Gaspar?

The Bible provides no names for the Wise Men, and so many attempts were made in the early centuries of Christianity to assign monikers. But it wasn't until a sixth-century Greek text, translated into Latin as *Excerpta Latina Barbari*, that they were given the names Melchior, Balthazar, and Gaspar — the names that have endured to this day.

What nativity story sites can be found in Bethlehem?

The most famous nativity story site is the Church of the Nativity. The church stands on a site that early Christians claimed was the site of Jesus' birth. When Rome began observing Christmas as a holiday, a church was built on the site.

In addition, there are three different locations that are said to be the site of the field where the shepherds were visited by the Angel of the Lord and told of the birth of Jesus. All faiths agree the site was east of Bethlehem, but Catholic, Protestant, and Orthodox churches can't agree on which field is *the* field.

What is the Epiphany?

The Epiphany, no matter which branch of Christianity you ask, takes place sometime shortly after Christmas. But the Eastern and Western churches differ on what the Epiphany represents. For Eastern churches, the Epiphany represents the day on which Jesus was baptized. For Western churches, the Epiphany celebrates the arrival of the three kings.

The exact day the Epiphany is observed varies. While the date of the Epiphany is January 6, the observation generally takes place on a Sunday. In the United States, the Epiphany is observed on the Sunday after the first Saturday in January; in England, it is observed on either January 6 or the Sunday between January 2 and 8.

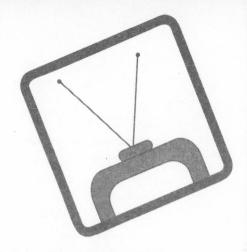

Movies, TV & Books

What was the first Christmas movie?

While it is difficult to know for certain what films may have been lost without a trace from the early days of film, the earliest Christmas-themed movie that we can point to was the 1897 film *Santa Claus Filling Stockings*. The film was a short one — mere minutes long — and the title also serves as a fairly thorough plot summary. But the film did end in spectacular fashion with Santa vanishing up a chimney — a special effect that would have amazed early filmgoers.

Is it true that Clement C. Moore didn't write "The Night Before Christmas"?

Originally titled "A Visit from Saint Nicholas," the classic poem first appeared in the December 23, 1823, edition of the *Troy Sentinel*. The newspaper claimed not to know who the author was. In 1837 — after the poem had enjoyed fourteen years of immense popularity — Clement C. Moore took credit for its writing.

Later, however, a woman who had been a governess at the Moore home claimed that she had received a handwritten copy of the poem from its true author, Henry Livingston Jr., and had given it to the Moore children.

Today, most dismiss the governess's story and accept Moore as the poem's author, but there are still many people who support the Livingston claim.

When was the first film version of *A Christmas Carol* made?

Dickens's classic novel first made its way onto the silver screen in 1901 with a British release, *Scrooge: Or, Marley's Ghost*. The film was eleven minutes long and was directed by W.R. Booth, though little else is known about the production or the cast. The ghosts of Christmases Past, Present, and Yet to Come are not part of the film: Scrooge's only ghostly visitor is Marley.

Over the years, *A Christmas Carol* has been filmed and refilmed more often than any other Christmas tale. The best-known versions are the 1951 British version starring Alastair Sim and the 1984 made-for-TV American version starring George C. Scott. Other versions have featured dogs, Muppets, Disney characters, former Starship *Enterprise* commanders, and, on one occasion, impressionist Rich Little playing every single character.

How many ghosts visit Scrooge in Charles Dickens's novel *A Christmas Carol*?

Strictly speaking, only four ghosts actually visit Scrooge. In addition to the ghosts of

The Ghosts of *Christmas Carols* Past

Some memorable movie versions of *A Christmas Carol*:

1901: *Scrooge: Or, Marley's Ghost* (first film version)

1908: *A Christmas Carol* (Thomas Ricketts)

1935: *Scrooge* (Seymour Hicks)

1938: *A Christmas Carol* (Reginald Owen)

1951: *Scrooge* (Alistair Sim)

1962: *Mr. Magoo's Christmas Carol* (animated, made-for-TV)

1970: *Scrooge* (Albert Finney, musical)

1975: *The Passions of Carol* (adult film)

1979: *An American Christmas Carol* (Henry Winkler, made-for-TV)

1983: *Mickey's Christmas Carol* (animated, made-for-TV)

1984: *A Christmas Carol* (George C. Scott, made-for-TV)

1988: *Scrooged* (Bill Murray)

1992: *A Muppet Christmas Carol* (Kermit the Frog and Michael Caine)

1999: *A Christmas Carol* (Patrick Stewart, made-for-TV)

2004: *A Christmas Carol: The Musical* (Kelsey Grammer, musical, made-for-TV)

Christmases Past, Present, and Yet to Come, the ghost of Marley visits. But Scrooge also witnesses a legion of other spirits when Marley directs Scrooge's attention to a poor woman and her child in the laneway, surrounded by lost souls who are trying to offer financial aid, but, being dead, failing in the effort.

How many Christmas books did Charles Dickens write?

Charles Dickens was something of a Christmas nut, and wrote Christmas chapters and stories into many of his books. Three books, however, were devoted exclusively to the holiday season: *The Chimes* (1844), *The Cricket on the Hearth* (1845), and, of course, *A Christmas Carol* (1843).

When did TV stations start broadcasting a burning log on Christmas Day?

In 1966, WPIX in New York City came up with the idea of pre-empting regular broadcasting and instead showing a log burning in a fireplace. You'd never see the log burn to ashes — the station aired a continuous seventeen-second loop. WPIX ended the tradition in 1990.

But it seems the public never stopped longing for the log, and over the next decade, log fans clamoured for its return. WPIX finally relented in 2001, and the log has been going strong ever since. In fact, it has spawned numerous imitators, with burning logs popping up on Christmas-morning television all over North America. Now, you can buy DVDs of burning logs, complete with crackling sounds and optional Christmas tunes. In recent years, one digital TV channel has begun broadcasting an interactive log that you can view from the angle of your choice.

When did the British monarchy first broadcast their annual Christmas message?

In 1932, George V finally accepted an invitation from the BBC that had been sent his way for nine years, and broadcast the first Royal Christmas Message on the radio. The King's message that year was written for him by Rudyard Kipling.

Ever since, every Christmas Day the reigning British monarch has delivered a message to the Commonwealth. The tradition moved from radio to television with Elizabeth II's 1957 broadcast. While the messages were originally delivered live at 3 p.m. GMT, since 1960 they have been pre-recorded and aired at times chosen by individual broadcasters.

Who wrote the story
"A Child's Christmas in Wales"?

Dylan Thomas originally began the story that evolved into "A Child's Christmas in Wales" as a 1945 radio broadcast for the BBC. Two years later, he wrote a piece called "A Conversation about Christmas" for *Picture Post*. Then, in 1950, he combined the two earlier stories into a piece for *Harper's Bazaar*. Eventually, even that version of the story was altered and broadcast on BBC Radio in 1952. This version was published as a book in 1954, a year after Thomas's death, and is the version we know today. The story lives on, not only in book form, but in annual re-airings of Thomas's 1952 broadcast and in a made-for-TV version co-produced by BBC and CBC, starring Denholm Elliott.

When was Bing Crosby's first Christmas special?

Bing Crosby became associated with Christmas through movies and songs, but he became a holiday institution with his annual Christmas specials. The first specials were actually broadcast on radio in 1935. In 1962, things moved to television, and Bing continued to entertain viewers until the final special — pre-recorded earlier that year — aired in December 1977, two months after Crosby passed away.

How many Christmas specials did Rankin and Bass produce?

The creative team of Arthur Rankin Jr. and Jules Bass was responsible for numerous Christmas specials using both conventional animation and stop-motion animation with figurines. If we include Thanksgiving and New Year's specials in our definition of "Christmas special," the duo gave us a total of nineteen holiday treats.

How many Christmas specials featured Charlie Brown and the Peanuts?

The 1965 special *A Charlie Brown Christmas* spawned numerous TV specials and television series featuring Charlie Brown and the

Rankin and Bass Christmas/Thanksgiving/ New Year's Specials:

- *Rudolph the Red-Nosed Reindeer* (1964)
- *The Cricket on the Hearth* (1967)
- *The Mouse on the Mayflower* (1968)
- *The Little Drummer Boy* (1968)
- *Frosty the Snowman* (1969)
- *Santa Claus is Comin' to Town* (1970)
- *'Twas the Night Before Christmas* (1974)
- *The Year Without a Santa Claus* (1974)
- *The First Christmas* (1975)
- *Frosty's Winter Wonderland* (1976)
- *Rudolph's Shiny New Year* (1976)
- *The Little Drummer Boy, Book II* (1976)
- *Nestor, The Long-Eared Christmas Donkey* (1977)
- *The Stingiest Man in Town* (1978)
- *Rudolph and Frosty's Christmas in July* (1979)
- *Pinocchio's Christmas* (1980)
- *The Leprechaun's Christmas Gold* (1981)
- *The Life and Adventures of Santa Claus* (1985)
- *Santa Baby* (2001)

Peanuts. But it wasn't until 1992 that we saw another Christmas-specific special: *It's Christmastime Again, Charlie Brown*. After the death of Peanuts creator Charles M. Schulz in 2000, two more Peanuts Christmas specials were created and aired: *Charlie Brown's Christmas Tales* (2002), and *I Want a Dog for Christmas, Charlie Brown* (2003).

If we include Thanksgiving (1973's *A Charlie Brown Thanksgiving*) and New Year's (1985's *Happy New Year, Charlie Brown*), the total Peanut holiday output comes to six.

Quickies

Did you know ...

- that *A Christmas Story* was the inspiration for the long-running television series *The Wonder Years*?
- that the first episode of *The Simpsons* was a Christmas special?
- that the classic 1970s television series *The Waltons* began as a one-off made-for-TV movie, *The Homecoming*?
- that the first live broadcast from lunar orbit occurred on Christmas Eve 1968, when Apollo 8 circled the moon?
- that Cary Grant was originally slated to star in *It's a Wonderful Life*?
- that *The Polar Express* was the first Christmas movie that had a 3D version?

How many TV specials featured Dr. Seuss's Grinch?

While the Grinch is best known for his starring role in *How the Grinch Stole Christmas* (1966), he returned to television in 1977's *Halloween Is Grinch Night*, and again in 1982's *The Grinch Grinches the Cat in the Hat*.

Who sang "You're a Mean One, Mr. Grinch" in the cartoon *How the Grinch Stole Christmas*?

While Boris Karloff provided the narration and the voice of the Grinch in the 1966 animated holiday classic, the song "You're a Mean One, Mr. Grinch" was sung by voiceover veteran Thurl Ravenscroft. Although Ravenscroft had a good deal of success doing voicework for the Grinch special and for a number of Disney animated features, he is best known as the voice of Tony the Tiger, the cartoon frontman for Kellogg's Frosted Flakes.

What was the first one-off Christmas television special?

On Christmas Day 1950, at 4 p.m., *One Hour in Wonderland* took to the airwaves. It was not only the first one-off Christmas special but also the first TV effort by Walt Disney. The special introduced us to members of Walt's family and featured a guest appearance by Edgar Bergen with Charlie McCarthy. More than just a holiday offering, the special served as an opportunity for Disney to plug its upcoming animated feature *Alice in Wonderland*, which would be released in 1951.

Was there really a Red Ryder BB gun?

In *A Christmas Story*, young Ralphie's "Holy Grail" of Christmas presents is the Red Ryder BB gun. Red Ryder was not a creation of the film's makers; he was a popular comic book hero, and his BB gun, produced by the Daisy Manufacturing Company, was a major hit in the 1940s.

However, the Red Ryder BB gun in *A Christmas Story* was actually invented for the film. Jean Shepherd, whose stories were used to create the script for the film, insisted that the Red Ryder BB gun he remembered had a sundial and compass on the stock. When the producers of the film asked Daisy to supply them with the gun, they were told that such a gun never existed. The sundial and compass were actually on another model, the Buck Jones Pump Gun. But the producers wanted the gun Shepherd had written — whether it had ever really existed or not — and so Daisy built a Red Ryder gun with the special Buck Jones features.

Who were the Knickerbockers and how did they influence the celebration of Christmas?

Formed in the early 1800s, the Knickerbockers were a patriotic group of American men of letters and included the likes of Washington Irving, Clement C. Moore, James

Fennimore Cooper, and John Pintard. Their name was derived from Irving's book *Diedrich Knickerbocker's History of New York*. The group took a particular interest in Christmas and made a largely successful attempt to influence an American version of Christmas that would be free from British trappings. Their most successful Americanization of the holiday was the creation of a new holiday gift-bringer: Santa Claus.

Did the movie *Holiday Inn* inspire the hotel chain?

While the Holiday Inn hotel chain owes its name to the 1942 Bing Crosby film, it would be inaccurate to say the real-life chain was inspired by the inn in the film.

Kemmons Wilson, seeing a need for an affordable, quality, family hotel chain on America's roadsides, launched Holiday Inn in 1952. The name was one that was only jokingly suggested to him by his architect in reference to the Crosby classic.

Who wrote the original story of *The Nutcracker*?

E.T.A. Hoffman, a nineteenth-century German writer and composer, wrote the story "The Nutcracker and the Mouse King" in 1816, introducing us to the nutcracker doll who magically comes to life and takes us to a world of living dolls.

Tchaikovsky set the story to music for the ballet *The Nutcracker* in 1892, and today it is enjoyed by families around the world at Christmastime.

Carols & Other Music

Where does the word *carol* come from?

The word *carol* first appeared in the English language in the fourteenth century. It is believed to have come from the Greek word *choros*, which refers to an activity involving singing and dancing in a circle. How the word became exclusively associated with Christmas songs is not known.

How much would it cost to buy all the gifts in "The Twelve Days of Christmas"?

PNC Wealth Management created its Christmas Price Index in 1985. The Christmas Price Index is a lighthearted annual report that updates us on the current cost of purchasing all the gifts listed in the song "The Twelve Days of Christmas."

In 2006, the total bill came to US$18,920.59.

This does not include the cost of housing and feeding the fifty humans and twenty-three birds that turn up under the unwitting recipient's tree. It's unlikely that pawning the five gold rings would cover such expenses. Presumably, "True Love" will be hearing about those costs for years to come.

What are the twelve days of Christmas?

The twelve days of Christmas are the twelve days between Christmas Day and the beginning of the Epiphany (which is either the day the Wise Men arrived or the day Jesus was baptized, depending on which branch of Christianity you ask). When the "twelve days" begin differs from country to country. Some countries begin the twelve days on Christmas Day, making the twelfth day the day before the Epiphany. Others exclude Christmas and begin counting on December 26, making the Epiphany the twelfth day.

To add to the confusion, in England, January 5 is the twelfth day of Christmas, and yet, January 6 is celebrated as "Twelfth Night."

What is the song "I Saw Three Ships" about?

"I Saw Three Ships" was written in the fifteenth century by an unknown author, and ever since, it has baffled anyone trying to determine what it is about. After all, it's unlikely that three ships "sailed into Bethlehem" on Christmas Day as the song says, given that there are no seas around Bethlehem for ships to sail in on.

The best guess seems to be that the song is a cryptic reference to the Three Kings — and, more specifically, the supposed arrival of their bodies in Cologne. Remains said to be the bones of the Three Kings had rested in Milan since A.D. 344. Holy Roman Emperor Frederick Barbarossa removed the remains and presented them to the Archbishop of Cologne in 1164. To this day, the remains are part of a shrine to the Three Kings at the Cologne Cathedral.

Was "Jingle Bells" originally written for Christmas?

Originally titled "One Horse Open Sleigh," "Jingle Bells" is an unusual Christmas song in that it makes no mention of Christmas — it simply celebrates a wintertime sleigh ride. The song was written by James Pierpont for a children's Sunday school pageant. But the occasion was not Christmas: it was a Thanksgiving pageant. The wintry theme ultimately tied it to Christmas, and it is now likely the best known of all Christmas songs.

Interestingly, there has been some dispute over where Pierpont composed the tune. While Medford, Massachusetts, laid claim to the tune for many years, the residents of balmy Savannah, Georgia, claim that the wintry song originated in their city. We do know that "Jingle Bells" was copyrighted in 1857, when Pierpont lived in Savannah, but we don't know for certain whether he wrote the song that year or many years earlier while living in Massachusetts.

Who wrote "Do They Know It's Christmas"?

Bob Geldof, the lead singer of one-hit wonders the Boomtown Rats, rose from semi-obscurity to music legend by putting together Band-Aid, a collection of Britain's most famous musical acts. Band-Aid recorded "Do They Know It's Christmas" in 1984 to raise money to aid famine victim in Ethiopia.

But while Geldof was the driving force behind the project, he was not the sole author of the song itself. Geldof co-wrote the tune with Midge Ure, best known for his work with the band Ultravox.

Who was "Good King Wenceslas"?

Wenceslas, as it turns out, wasn't a king, but a Bohemian duke in the tenth century. Wenceslas was known for his good deeds and was canonized following his death. In 1853, one story of Wenceslas's kindness inspired J.M. Neale to pen the lyrics for the classic carol. The story told of a night when Wenceslas and his page, in an effort to feed and warm a peasant, battled a raging snowstorm. When the page was unable to continue any further, Wenceslas advised him to walk in the duke's footsteps.

The "feast of Stephen" referred to in the song is St. Stephen's Day, December 26.

How many times did Bing Crosby sing "White Christmas" in a movie?

Bing Crosby first brought Irving Berlin's "White Christmas" to the big screen in the 1942 film *Holiday Inn*. The song went on to become the best selling Christmas recording of all time. He performed the tune again in the 1946 release *Blue Skies*. Then, in 1954, the studio clearly thought moviegoers had not had enough of the song, and Bing again sang his signature ditty on screen — this time, they used the song's name as the title of the film.

Did King George really begin the tradition of standing for the Hallelujah Chorus of Handel's *Messiah*?

According to legend, the tradition of standing for the Hallelujah Chorus in Handel's *Messiah* began when King George II was so moved by the emotional power of the music that he leapt to his feet, prompting all those in attendance to do the same.

Strictly speaking, there's no evidence that George ever attended a performance of *Messiah*. However, the legend continues, as does the tradition of standing.

How long did it take Handel to compose *Messiah*?

George Frideric Handel's massive oratorio, when played in its entirety, runs for roughly three hours. But the task of writing *Messiah* took a surprisingly short period of time. Handel began work on *Messiah* on August 22, 1741, and finished on September 14 — a mere twenty-three days later.

> **Quickies**
> *Did you know ...*
> • that since 2001, according to the American Society of Composers, Artists, and Publishers (ASCAP), the most-played Christmas recording on American radio is the Nat King Cole rendition of "The Christmas Song (Chestnuts Roasting on an Open Fire)"?
> • that according to ASCAP, the Christmas song that has been recorded more times than any in history is "White Christmas," with more than five hundred versions?

Interestingly, while *Messiah* has become a staple of the Christmas season, it was not meant for Christmas performance. Handel wrote it for Easter, and the first performance took place on April 13, 1742, at Neal's Music Hall in Dublin, Ireland.

What does "Auld Lang Syne" mean?

Much of the planet sings "Auld Lang Syne" at Christmas and New Year's without having a clue what the words *auld lang syne* actually mean.

The lyrics for the song were written by Scots poet Robbie Burns, who wrote much of his work in Gaelic. The phrase *auld lang syne* directly translates to "old long since," which can more accurately be read as "times gone by."

Who wrote the song "Rudolph the Red-Nosed Reindeer"?

Johnny Marks took the popular Christmas story and turned it into a song in 1947. For the next two years, however, he struggled to find a singer willing to record the song, until Gene Autry took a chance and turned "Rudolph" into a classic.

Marks went on to write a number of popular Christmas songs, including "Rockin' Around the Christmas Tree" and "A Holly Jolly Christmas."

What was the best selling Christmas album of all time?

With 12 million units sold worldwide, Mariah Carey's 1994 album *Merry Christmas* has sold more than any other Christmas album in history.

Gift-Giving & Cards

When was the first Christmas card created?

Christmas cards followed the lead of Valentine's Day cards, which had become popular in the 1820s. The first known Christmas card appeared in 1843. Commissioned by Henry Cole and illustrated by John Calcott Horsley, the card showed a family enjoying their holiday punch. The simple inscription on the card said, "A Merry Christmas and a Happy New Year to You."

One thousand copies of the card were produced and sent to Cole's friends and family.

What was the first Christmas stamp?

While Christmas stamps didn't catch on worldwideuntil the middle of the twentieth century, the earliest Christmas stamp was produced in Canada in 1898. The stamp featured a map of the world and the words "XMAS 1898."

How did the Christmas seals tradition begin?

Christmas seals were the brainchild of postal clerk Einar Holbøll of Denmark, who had become dismayed at the number of children dying from tuberculosis. Seeing the large volume of mail coming through his place of work each day, he came up with the idea of selling seals to raise money to help eradicate the disease. The postmaster agreed, and the first Christmas seals were produced in 1904. Within a few years, the idea caught hold in the United States, where its cause was championed by Emily Bissell.

How much does the average person spend on Christmas gifts?

It's no secret that Christmas is the biggest time of year for retailers, with many basing their entire year's success or failure on Christmas revenues. As customers, we're clearly doing our part to help them out. Recent studies have shown that in the United Kingdom, the average consumer spends £300 on gifts during the holiday season. In Canada, the number is close to C$700, and in the United States, US$800.

How much online shopping do people do at Christmas?

In the early days of Internet retailing, security concerns kept many people from sharing credit card information online. But in recent years, the ease of online shopping has led to a huge increase in Internet sales. In the period leading up to Christmas in 2006, Americans spent $24.6 billion online, up 26 percent over the previous year. In the U.K., £4.98 billion was spent — a 51 percent increase from 2005.

Who spends more on gifts — men or women?

In annual surveys conducted by Deloitte & Touche in the U.K., it has been shown that women will spend more overall on gifts, but there are differences in how each gender spends their money. Women tend to spend more money on clothes and, in the case of mothers, spend more money on their daughters. Men spend more money on socializing and on their partners. As far as *receiving* gifts goes, fathers and sons are left out in the cold, as more money is spent — by both genders — on mothers, daughters, and female partners.

What was the best selling toy of all time?

While there have been a number of toy crazes during the holiday season — from the hula hoop, to Cabbage Patch Kids, to computer gaming consoles — the best selling toy of all time is that maddening block of movable squares, Rubik's cube. Rubik's cube and its imitators have sold more than 300 million units globally since the puzzle was introduced in 1980.

How many Christmas cards are sent each year?

While there are no reliable estimates on the number of electronic greeting cards that are sent, the traditional Christmas card is thriving. In the United States, 2 billion cards are sent each year.

Reindeer & Elves

Are Santa's reindeer male or female?

If we believe the images of the reindeer on Christmas cards and in movies, then Santa's sleigh is pulled by female reindeer. Reindeer are the only deer species in which both males and females have antlers. But Christmas falls just after the reindeer breeding season, and it's at this time that the male antlers fall off.

The poor males, tired from the business of breeding and the ritual fighting with other males over potential mates, find that hormonal changes lead to bone reabsorption at the base of their antlers, and the old antlers fall off, leaving the lads antlerless for about four months.

When did we first hear the story of Rudolph the Red-Nosed Reindeer?

In 1939, Montgomery Ward department store in Chicago was looking for a Christmas promotion. They asked staff copywriter Robert Lewis May to produce a children's book that would be used as a giveaway. May came up with the story of an underappreciated red-nosed reindeer who became a hero on Christmas Eve. Originally, the reindeer was named "Rollo," until May's daughter suggested "Rudolph" would be a catchier moniker.

The book was a hit that year, and the store continued to give it away each Christmas season. In 1949, the little story became a hit song when Gene Autry recorded the Johnny Marks tune.

Who first named the reindeer?

We first learned the names of Santa's reindeer in a poem that is still one of the best-known pieces of Christmas literature: Clement C. Moore's "A Visit from St. Nicholas" (now most commonly referred to as "The Night Before Christmas").

In the poem, we witness Santa calling out his reindeer's names: Dasher, Dancer, Prancer, Vixen, Comet, Cupid, Donder, and Blitzen.

Why is Santa's seventh reindeer sometimes called "Donner" and sometimes "Donder"?

In the original publication of the poem in 1823, the seventh reindeer was actually neither "Donder" nor "Donner." He was "Dunder." And the eighth reindeer was named "Blixem."

When an 1837 version of the poem was being prepared for printing, the publisher changed "Dunder" to "Donder," and "Blixem" to "Blixen." (The latter change was made because "Blixen" made for a better rhyme with "Vixen.")

Then, in 1844, when Clement C. Moore was preparing the text for his publisher, he retained the earlier change to "Donder" and altered the eighth reindeer's name to "Blitzen." It's this version of the poem that became the standard.

Somewhere along the way, "Donder" became "Donner." While it's not quite clear when this change took place, many have pointed a finger at Robert L. May, the author of the original *Rudolph the Red-Nosed Reindeer* story. Johnny Marks and Gene Autry continued with the new name in the introductory verse of the song version of Rudolph's tale, and "Donner" soon became the standard. Reindeer purists tend to prefer Donder, however.

When did reindeer first begin pulling Santa's sleigh?

We first learned that Santa's sleigh was pulled by reindeer with the 1821 publication of *The Children's Friend: A New Year's Present, to Little Ones from Five to Twelve.*

> Old Santeclaus with much delight
> His reindeer drives this frosty night.
> O'er chimney tops, and tracks of snow,
> To bring his yearly gifts to you.

The little book doesn't tell us how many reindeer pull the sleigh, though the accompanying illustrations depict only one. The number of gifts Santa had to haul must have increased exponentially after the writing of the poem, because by the time "A Visit from St. Nicholas" was published just two years later, the team had expanded to eight reindeer.

How many reindeer would be required to pull enough toys to satisfy all the children in the world?

Assuming even a modest gift-giving season (each child receiving one two-pound gift), Santa's sleigh would weigh roughly 500,000 tons, which seems like a hard night's work for eight reindeer, even with Rudolph's help.

Reindeer are capable of pulling up to 300 pounds of toys (or other payloads), meaning that it would take 3,333,333 reindeer to pull Santa's sleigh when fully loaded.

And you thought remembering eight reindeer names was tough.

What is the difference between reindeer and caribou?

There are many who consider reindeer and caribou the same animal. And in fact, they share the same genus and species name: *Rangifer tarandus*. The distinction that is usually made is that reindeer are domesticated deer, while caribou are not. But those looking to make further distinctions point to a number of different traits. For example, reindeer are shorter and stouter than caribou. Also, reindeer have thicker fur than their caribou cousins. The naysayers attribute such differences to the domestication of reindeers and insist that while there are some differences, the two deer are virtually the same.

When were elves first credited with making Santa's toys?

Elves have been with us for centuries, though originally they were nasty, spiteful creatures, even at Christmas.

During the nineteenth century, that began to change. Santa himself was said to take the form of an elf ("A Visit from Saint Nicholas" refers to him as "a right jolly old elf"), and while he ultimately grew to full human size, the elf world was delighted to see that he didn't abandon his roots. In the 1860s, illustrator Thomas Nast — whose work in *Harper's Weekly* gave us much of our knowledge of Santa — depicted a North Pole workshop manned by toymaking elves.

Who are some of Santa's "helpers"?

In North America, Santa Claus is known to be helped by an unspecified number of helpers. But around the world, Santa, in his different forms, has a variety of sidekicks. St. Nicholas, for example, is accompanied by Zwarte Piet in the Netherlands. Pelznickel is the helper of choice in Germany. And when Nicholas arrives in Austria, Klaubauf is by his side.

These and other helpers tend to do Santa's dirty work for him. They dole out punishment through nasty treats or threats of capture. However, in some areas of Europe, Santa / Nicholas is accompanied by the Christ Child (often portrayed by a young girl).

Food & Drink

When were candy canes invented?

In the mid-seventeenth century, a choirmaster in the Cologne Cathedral was fed up with the noisemaking of children attending the church's nativity scene. Pleas for silence were fruitless, and so he came up with a foolproof plan: he made candy sticks and distributed them to the children. Too busy licking the delicious gift, the children were unable to create their usual ruckus.

In an inspired moment that would create a lasting symbol of the holiday season, the choirmaster curled the ends to make the candies resemble a shepherd's crook.

Candy canes underwent a dramatic change sometime around 1900. Prior to that time, the candies were completely white. In the early 1900s, stripes began to appear, and today, the idea of a candy cane without stripes is almost an abomination.

When did turkey become the traditional food of the Christmas feast?

Turkey, being a "new world" bird, has not always been tied to Christmas. But soon after William Strickland introduced the turkey to England in the sixteenth century, it began its rise to holiday prominence. Still, it was considered too expensive for most people, and roast beef and goose were more common. But towards the end of the nineteenth century, turkey took over as the traditional main course for Christmas dinners.

Meanwhile in North America, the turkey's native land, the turkey has always been the bird of choice.

How many turkeys are consumed at Christmas?

In the United Kingdom, 10 million turkeys meet their ultimate fate on the dinner tables of Christmas revellers each year. In the United States, 22 million turkeys become Christmas dinner. American turkeys have the misfortune of being hit twice at the end of the year, since turkey is also the traditional food of the Thanksgiving feast in late November. A whopping 46 million birds are consumed at American Thanksgiving dinners.

How long can you keep a fruitcake?

The polarizing fruitcake — loved by some and reviled by others — has some serious staying power. According to *The Joy of Cooking*, a fruitcake soaked in alcohol, buried in powdered sugar, and stored in an airtight tin can last up to twenty-five years.

Does flaming your plum pudding cause the alcohol to burn off?

The sight of a flaming pudding is one that many house-holds are familiar with at Christmas. But unfortunately — or fortunately, depending on your penchant for spirits — only about 20 percent of the alcohol will burn off before the flame dies out.

The notion that alcohol evaporates during any cooking process is also something of a myth. While it's true that a good deal of alcohol does burn off in cooking — due largely to the low boiling point of alcohol — anywhere from one-twentieth to half of the original alcohol will remain, depending on the cooking process involved.

When did the custom of leaving milk and cookies for Santa Claus begin?

The exact point at which the cookies-for-Santa tradition began is impossible to trace, but it's generally agreed that the custom began in the 1930s. Cookies were left both as a bribe (naughty boys and girls trying to sway Santa at the last minute) and a thank you (nice boys and girls expressing gratitude for the motherlode that would surely await them in the morning).

What is the most popular cookie to leave for Santa Claus?

There are no exact figures, and Santa isn't saying, but it seems reasonable to conclude that Oreos are filling Santa's ample belly more than any other cookie.

Since hitting the market in 1912, Oreo cookies have been the most popular cookie in the world, with between 350 and 400 billion biscuits being sold over the years, at a rate of more than 9 million annually.

It stands to reason, then, given the sheer number of cookies out there, that Oreos are waiting for Santa at more houses than other brands.

At press time, there was no word on whether Santa eats the middles first.

What is "nog"?

In the nineteenth century, American soldiers discovered that a popular drink made with eggs and milk could take on a more festive feel with the addition of rum. The word *nog*, which was another word for "ale," was applied to the concoction.

Quickies

Did you know ...

- that in the town of Oaxaca, Mexico, Christmas Eve is also known as "the Night of the Radishes"? Radishes are carved into various shapes and prizes are awarded.
- that a ban on alcohol during the 1826 Christmas season at West Point military academy sparked a night of violence that became known as the "Eggnog Riot"? Among the rioters was Jefferson Davis, who later became the first and only president of the Confederate States of America.

Is there really meat in "mincemeat"?

While vegetarian versions of mincemeat have turned the traditional recipe into a relic of the past for many people, true mincemeat really does contain meat — usually beef, as well as beef suet. Mincemeat was first developed as a means of preserving meat without smoking or salting it.